إِنَّ ٱللَّهَ وَمَلَـٰٓئِكَتَهُۥ يُصَلُّونَ عَلَى ٱلنَّبِىِّ ۚ يَـٰٓأَيُّهَا ٱلَّذِينَ ءَامَنُواْ صَلُّواْ عَلَيْهِ وَسَلِّمُواْ تَسْلِيمًا ﴿٥٦﴾

Indeed, Allāh and His angels send blessings upon the Prophet ﷺ. O you who have believed, ask [Allāh to send] blessings and peace upon him ﷺ.

Ref: Al-Qur'an Surat Al Ahzab 33:56

For Parents And Teachers

"To know a person is to learn and study the character of a person."

This book has been particularly compiled for the benefits of introducing our young readers to have a true and correct understanding of the Prophet and Messenger of God; Muhammad (pbuh) and to truly learn of his noble character, his special gifts and miracles graced by Almighty God Allah.

This book has been designed for the ages of between 7 and 12 years old who are able to read by themselves independently. However, by no means that this book is to be limited to those ages.

I encourage parents to read the book and to narrate to their children as young as 3 years old; perhaps at bed time or assigning a family time in some part of the days during the week by which everyone can interact and share their thoughts.

It is with intent and hope that this book is not only to be limited as a household possession, but will also make it's way towards educating the young learners/students both in the Islamic madrasah (schools) and the secular schools alike within their RE (religious education) subject when teaching and learning about Islam.

Ustadha Shareefah Al Husaini
Jan 2023

In loving memory of my beloved sister

I remember the day I told my beloved sister Anjum I would love to write a short story about Prophet Muhammad ﷺ (pbuh), and she said "go for it".

She introduced me to our beloved and blessed teacher Ustadha Shareefah, who has narrated this book, and so, we began our journey.

For you my dear sister, nothing was too difficult nor impossible, you were a brave soul who inspired me with your true faith and courage.

I hope this short message and this book inspire our young readers to be courageous and pursue their dreams while remaining true to themselves. Learning about and knowing the Prophet ﷺ (pbuh) is gaining closeness to our Creator.

Tasnim Ghumra
Jan 2023

His birth made clear the purity of his origin,
O how pure his beginning and his end!
Ref: The Burda, Imam Sharaf Ad-Din Al-Busiri

Contents

❦ Chapter 1 ❧
The Best of Allah's Creation

بِسْمِ اللهِ الرَّحْمٰنِ الرَّحِيْمِ

In the name of Allah, the most Gracious, the most Merciful

اللَّهُمَّ صَلِّ عَلَى مُحَمَّدٍ وَعَلَى آلِ مُحَمَّدٍ

O Allah! Send Your blessing to (the prophet) Muhammad and the progeny of Muhammad".

Allah the Almighty has granted His beloved Prophet Muhammad ﷺ (pbuh) an exalted status in this world and the hereafter. He ﷺ (pbuh) is "Al Mustafa" – the chosen one, Allah's Beloved.

Prophet Muhammad's ﷺ (pbuh) name is mentioned 4 times in the Qur'an. He ﷺ (pbuh) is called Ahmad (sallallahu alaihi wasallam), in the heavens and Muhammad (sallallahu alaihi wasallam) on earth. It is our duty to send salawat (blessings) upon Prophet Muhammad ﷺ (pbuh) if we want to gain closeness to Allah ﷻ (Subhanahu wa Ta'ala - Glorified and Exalted).

When the angels send blessings upon Prophet Muhammad ﷺ (pbuh), they implore God's blessings for him (pbuh) and his progeny.

The Islamic world uses the Islamic calendar also known as the Hijra calendar (Arabic: التقويم الهجري at-taqweem al-hijrī). It is a lunar calendar, which means the end and beginning of the month which depends on the sighting of the moon. Unlike the Gregorian calendar, the Islamic calendar has either 29 or 30 days in a month. There are 12 months and these are in the following order: Muharram, Safar, Rabi-Al-Awwal, Rabi-Al-Akhar, Jumada-Al-Awwal, Jumada-Al-Akhar, Rajab, Shaban, Ramadhan, Shawwal, Dhul Qa'dah and Dhul Hijjah.

Allah The Almighty sent The Prophet Muhammad ﷺ (pbuh) as a *"Mercy to the Worlds"* as described in the Qur'an. Therefore Prophet Muhammad ﷺ (pbuh) is the last Prophet sent by God. He ﷺ (pbuh) was born on Monday in the month of Rabi-Al-Awwal, in the year of the elephant, the 'Aam ul fil' in the city of Makkah.

Surah al Imran ayat 31 - command from Allah to Prophet Muhammad ﷺ, to tell the people who believe:

$$\text{قُلْ إِن كُنتُمْ تُحِبُّونَ ٱللَّهَ فَٱتَّبِعُونِي يُحْبِبْكُمُ ٱللَّهُ وَيَغْفِرْ لَكُمْ ذُنُوبَكُمْ ۗ وَٱللَّهُ غَفُورٌ رَّحِيمٌ ﴿٣١﴾}$$

Translation: "Say, if you (really) love Allah then follow me (ie accepting Islamic monotheism), Allah will love you, and forgive your sins; and Allah is oft forgiving and merciful".

Allah's love for His beloved Rasul ﷺ (pbuh) is unique that no other Prophets or Angels can reach this high status that Allah ﷻ (Glorified and Exalted) granted only to Prophet Muhammad ﷺ (pbuh). The station of Mahmoud (praiseworthy).

The Prophets ﷺ (pbuh) father's name was Abdullah bin Abd Al-Muttalib, and his mother's name was Aaminah. His grandfather was Abd Al-Muttalib and his uncle was Abu Talib, who was also the father of his cousin, Ali ﷺ

(r.a.), who later married Lady (Sayyidatuna) Fatima ﷺ (r.a.), (Prophets ﷺ (pbuh) daughter).
The Beloved Prophet Muhammad ﷺ (pbuh) was orphaned at the the age of 6.

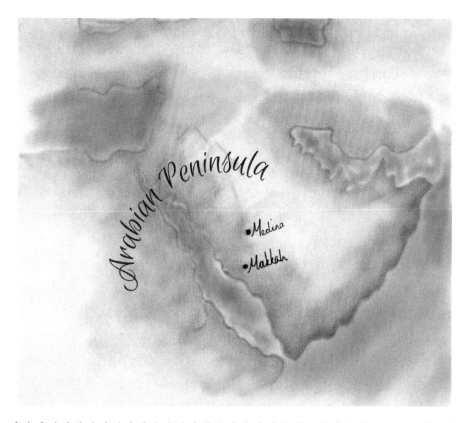

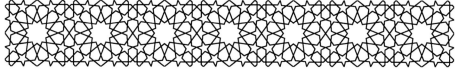

🦋 Chapter 2 🦋

The Miraculous Birth of
The Prophet ﷺ (pbuh)

It was a night filled with light, stars shining at their brightest in the infinite heavens, the luminous essence of nature showcasing its beauty. Something special was going to happen, a true joy, a true light was going to appear.

On this night, Almighty Allah blessed His creations with the presence of His Beloved, His Chosen One, Prophet Muhammad ﷺ (pbuh). It was either within the last hour or the last half an hour before Fajr, during the third of the night, that the Beloved Prophet ﷺ (pbuh) was born. There are several narrations by scholars describing this blissful and special event. On the night of the joyous and blessed birth of the Prophet's ﷺ (pbuh), his blessed mother Lady (Sayyidatuna) Aaminah witnessed the illumination of light extending to the palaces of Syria. And, on that night the whole house was illuminated with light upon light.
Ref: The Morning of Light, al karma publications

From this we can see that this was no ordinary birth –
an arrival, indeed, of the Light of Guidance from the
Lord of the Worlds.

Although historians differ with regards to the dates the
Prophet ﷺ (pbuh) was born, the 12th of Rabi-al-awwal
is the date agreed by most of the ancient prophetic
biographers, scholars of the science and prophetic
traditions, scholars of Quranic explanation, people of
the second generation after the Prophet ﷺ (pbuh) and
the noble prophetic companions.

The same year is also known as the year of the
elephant, the 'Aam ul Fil' as another historical event
took place in that year. It was when the governor of
Yemen, Abraha, with his troops and elephants rode
towards Makkah to destroy the Holy Kaa'ba. As they
marched towards the city of Makkah, Abd Al-Muttalib
caught sight of a giant cloud of dust and sand
approaching him from a distance, he at once knew that
it was the army of Abraha, wanting to ruin the Kaa'ba.
Abd Al-Muttalib held the door of the Kaa'ba and
prayed intensely to Allah Almighty to save the Kaa'ba
from the evil intentions of Abraha. Miraculously,
Almighty Allah sent down birds carrying little stones by

their beaks to rain on Abraha and his army and they were all killed.

He ﷺ (pbuh) was also reported to have been born 50 days after the incident of the elephant on Monday the 12th of Rabi ul Awwal according to Ibn Khaldun in Tarikh ibn Khaldun. It was also the 40th year of the rule of Anushirvan (who was Khosrau 1 of Persia). Therefore this is an especially important and auspicious time for all Muslims around the world, a time that takes them back to the memory of the one who led humanity from darkness to light; and who is described by Allah as "a Mercy to the worlds".

The Prophet ﷺ (pbuh) was sent by Allah as a blessing for the whole universe, not just one nation, but every nation; regardless of race and creed.

Allah Almighty, the Most Wise, commands us to follow the footsteps of the best of creation, Prophet Muhammad ﷺ (pbuh).

"And indeed, you are surely on an excellent standard of character".

Ref: Qur'an, Chapter 68: Verse 4

Al-Shifa' bint 'Awf was the sister of Abd al-Rahman ibn 'Awf, one of the first eight people who accepted Islam. Al-Shifa' bint 'Awf was the wet nurse who helped Lady

8

Aaminah deliver the Prophet ﷺ (pbuh). As she held the Prophet ﷺ (pbuh) in her two hands she heard a voice addressing her "Your Lord have mercy upon You".
Ref: Prophetic Biography Seerat Diya' Al-Nabi

Indeed, it was the voices of angels proclaiming their joy, and blessings upon her! What a sight this must have been to behold! That moment of joy, blessing, celebration, an event so wonderful and blessed by Allah Almighty the Majestic. The light of Allah radiates through His beloved Messenger spreading into the darkness of the night.

As the mother of the Prophet ﷺ (pbuh) Lady Aaminah was lying down, darkness spread, she trembled with fear in bewilderment. Suddenly a light appeared to the right, someone asked "where did you take this child"? A voice answered, "I took him to the West". Then there was darkness again, and she shivered with fear, another light appeared, this time to her left, and another voice asked, "where did you take him?"; a voice replied "I took him to the East and I will not take him again".

We now know that this was no ordinary birth, but a gift from God as a Mercy to the Worlds.

We also learn from further narrations that the Prophet's ﷺ (pbuh) uncle Sayyidina 'Abbas ﷛ (r.a.) states that the Prophet ﷺ (pbuh) was already circumcised and that his umbilical cord was already cut. The Prophet ﷺ (pbuh) arrived into this world with such magnificence and dignity, an honour Allah ﷻ (Glorified and Exalted) has given to His most beloved of creation.

Allah Almighty had already informed Prophet Moses عليه السلام (a.s.) of the birth of the Prophet ﷺ (pbuh). Prophet Moses عليه السلام (a.s.) informed his nation Bani Israel (Children of Israel), "when a (certain) star will move from its place, that will be the time of the birth of the last prophet". This information was passed from generation to generation of the Bani Israel, who eagerly awaited the news of the birth of the last prophet. As is famously mentioned in the Torah (book of the Jews), and in the Injeel (Bible).

The night that Muhammad ﷺ (pbuh) was born, Allah Almighty, The Exalted, commanded the angels to open wide all the gates of Paradise. On this auspicious day the sun shone with more brilliance, its light greater than any other days, and the whole world was radiant and luminous.

Another event relating to the blessed birth of the
Prophet ﷺ (pbuh) in Makkah took place as follows:

A Jew who resided in Makkah went to a gathering of the Quraish and asked them, "has a child been born amongst you tonight?", he also told the Quraish: "remember my words! in this night the Prophet of the last community (Ummah) will be born, and O Quraish! he will be from your tribe, and there will be some hair in one place on his shoulder". After the Quraish had heard what the Jew had said, they all departed to their homes and asked their family members, if a child had been born. They were informed that indeed, this night a son has been born to Abdullah ibn Abd Al-Muttalib, and he has been given the blessed name of Muhammad.

The people went to the Jew to tell him, that he was correct, that a child had been born to the Quraish. The Jew immediately asked to be taken to see the baby, Muhammad ﷺ (pbuh). He was brought to the home of Lady Aaminah, the blessed mother of the Prophet ﷺ (pbuh). The Jew requested for Lady Aaminah to show him her son. She brought her blessed child, they removed the covering, and when the Jew saw the spot of hair on the Prophet ﷺ (pbuh) as described in the Torah, he fainted and fell to the ground!!!

When the Jew regained consciousness, the people who were with him, asked as to what happened to him. The

Jew then replied with such regret, "Prophethood has ended from the Children of Israel." The Jew then went on to address the people of Quraish, "O tribe of Quraish! Rejoice and celebrate, due to the blessedness of this fortunate newborn, your honour and greatness shall spread throughout the East and West."
Ref: Ibid

There were miracles after miracles that occurred on this extremely beautiful night. We learn from one narration that Abd Al-Muttalib mentioned, "that night I was in the Ka'ba, and all the idols fell down into prostration".

Another narration states that all the animals of the Quraish talked that night: "We swear by the Lord of the Ka'ba that the Prophet is coming – who is the guardian/protector of the entire world and is the sun of its people (shedding the light of guidance)."
Ref: Al-Khasais al-Kubra with reference to Abu Nu'aym from ibn 'Abbās Radi Allahu Anhu

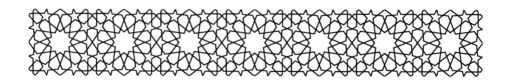

❧ Chapter 3 ❧

Actions and Mannerisms

❈Manners of Eating and drinking by the Prophet ﷺ (pbuh)

Prophet Muhammad ﷺ (pbuh) taught us the adaab (manners) of eating. As Muslims we hope to perform all our actions according to the way the Prophet ﷺ (pbuh) did in his lifetime.

The sunnah is to eat with minimum of three fingers although it is permissible to eat with all five fingers depending on the type of food we are eating.

The Prophet ﷺ (pbuh) forbade us from eating with two fingers for he said, "this is a trait of the devil" (shaytan). Prophet Muhammad ﷺ (pbuh) also forbade us from eating and drinking with our left hand for the devil eats and drinks with the left hand. We should not eat and drink to fill ourselves, rather we should eat and drink in moderation, as instructed by Rasulullah (Messenger of God) ﷺ (pbuh); in consideration of 1/3 of food; 1/3 of water; leaving 1/3 for air.

Over-indulging which is too much eating and drinking, could cause physical illnesses, coarseness in the self and dullness in the brain. Here, we learn from the teachings of the Prophet ﷺ (pbuh) that we should eat to live and not live to eat. Therefore, we should follow the etiquette of eating for no-one enjoys eating with people who eat greedily.

✿The sunnah (Prophetic way) of eating:

- wash our hands before eating
- recite Bismillah or du'a (supplication) before eating
- eat and drink with the right hand
- eat food that is the nearest to you as the blessing on the food is in the middle of the plate, which is to be left till the end.
- The Prophet ﷺ (pbuh) said, to pick up any food that has dropped (still edible), remove the dirt from it and eat it, and not leave it to the devil.
- The Prophet ﷺ (pbuh) taught us to lick our fingers after our meals, and wipe our plates clean with our

fingers, because he ﷺ (pbuh) said "you never know in which part of our food the blessing (barakah) lies".
Ref: Sahih Muslim

✽The sunnah (Prophetic way) of drinking:
- recite Bismillah (with the name of God)
- do not drink in one gulp.
- drink in 2 or 3 sips at a time and pause for breath between sips.
- recite Alhamdulillah (All Praise is to God) when you finish
  Ref: Al Tirmidhi
- when sharing a drink, the cup should be handed to the one on the right, then the one to his right and continue in the same manner.
  Ref: Al Bukhari and Muslim

✽On Entering and Leaving the house:
On entering the home Rasulullah ﷺ (pbuh) taught us to enter with our right foot whilst saying "Bismillah hir-rahman nir-raheem". This is to ensure that the devil does not follow us into the house. Then, to say "Assalamu'alaykum" to the people in the house. When leaving the house we are to step out with our left foot, and to read 'Bismillahi tawakkaltu 'allallah; wala haula wala quwwata illa billah"; "in the name of Allah, most

Compassionate, most Merciful, I put my trust, and there is no success except with Allah".

Similarly, we are to wear our shoes beginning with our right foot, followed by the left, and do the opposite when taking off our shoes starting with the left foot followed by the right. These principles of starting from the right preceding over the left is to be applied to all our daily actions, such as when putting on and taking off our clothes, socks, gloves, etc.

However, there is one exception, which is when entering the bathroom and lavatory, one needs to enter with the left foot whilst reading the du'a for Allah's protection from the devil (shaytan) and leaving the bathroom and lavatory with the right foot while reading the du'a of gratitude to Allah after relieving oneself.

These examples are by no means exhausted, and we encourage our readers and parents to learn and develop their understanding and perform their lifestyle habits according to the Sunnah (practices) of the Prophet ﷺ (pbuh).

❋Manners of sitting in accordance with the sunnah (Prophetic way) of the Prophet ﷺ (pbuh):

Do not sit between two people without their permission, rather sit to their left or their right. Abu Daud reported that RasulAllah ﷺ (pbuh) said, "no one is to sit between two people without their permission".

When you are given permission to sit between two people, be grateful and be good mannered towards their kind gesture by thanking them; do not sit cross-legged to crowd them out causing them discomfort. A wise man once said, "two people are truly ungrateful: a person to whom you give advice and he hates you for it, and a person who is favoured with a seat in a tight place and he sits cross-legged".
Ref: Hafidh Sam'aani, Adaab al-Imala wal-Istimla

When sitting between two people or amongst a few do not eavesdrop and listen to their conversations or to what they are saying, as their conversations could be confidential or private. Eavesdropping is a very bad habit. The Prophet ﷺ (pbuh) said, "whoever listens to peoples' conversations against their wishes will be

punished by liquid lead being poured down their ears on the day of judgement."
Ref: Bukhari; Sahih

We should aim to sit in the company of the elders so that we benefit from their wisdom.

Another important point to note is that it is bad manners to whisper to someone when you are in a group of three. This is because the third person will feel excluded and ignored and will feel hurt by your behaviour. So, we have to be careful not to behave in this manner. The Prophet ﷺ (pbuh) said "no two (people) shall exchange whispers in
the presence of a third person."
Ref: Imam Malik and Abu Daud

In another version The Prophet ﷺ (pbuh) said, "if you were three, two of you should not whisper to each other, till you join other people, lest the third feel offended."
Ref: Bukhari

We now know that such behaviour mentioned above is not only forbidden but is also despicable. Abdullah ibn

Umar ﷺ (r.a. Radiiallahu Anhu - May Allah be pleased with him) was asked, "what if there were four?" He answered, "than it does not matter," meaning it is not offensive because the third person has another person to talk to. Whispers are often secrets, so if someone whispers to you, you are entrusted with a secret, do not betray it; not even to your best friend or closest relative.

It is important for us to take guidance from the above teachings of the Prophet ﷺ (pbuh).

❋Manners of sleeping in accordance with the sunnah (Prophetic way) of the Prophet ﷺ (pbuh):

- perform ablution (wudu')
- to lie down on your right side (Prophet ﷺ (pbuh) also used to place his hand under his right cheek, and say the following prayer).

Du'a (supplication) when going to sleep
Allahumma bismika amutu wa ahya -
O'Allah In your name I die, and I live

Du' a (supplication) when waking up

Alhamdu lillahil ladhi ahyana ba'da ma amatana wa ilayhin-nushur

All praise belongs to the one who gave us life after he had given us death and to him is the resurrection.

• do not lie down on your belly. The Prophet ﷺ (pbuh) said "Allah dislikes this way of lying down".
Ref: Abu Daud

❋Etiquette of speaking and meeting people taught by the Prophet ﷺ (pbuh):

The Prophet ﷺ (pbuh) taught us to speak with a pleasant tone of voice, to speak softly yet clearly. Raising your voice is against good manners, and shows a lack of respect for the person to whom we are talking to. We must maintain this behaviour with our friends, strangers, the young and especially the old. More so, it is most important to speak with a pleasant tone of voice, good and kind words, pleasant and gentle look on our faces when addressing parents, grandparents, and people whose status demands great respect: i.e. teachers, especially religious teachers and leaders.

This behaviour will in turn earn you respect because if you give respect you gain respect.

❧ Chapter 4 ❧
Wives of the Prophet ﷺ (pbuh)

✹Umm al Mu'mineen – Mothers of the Believers

The Prophet's ﷺ (pbuh) wives known as the "Mothers of the Believers" preceded all women. Allah ﷻ (Glorified and Exalted) has given women a high status, an elevated status whether she is a daughter, a sister, a wife or a mother. The Mothers of the Believers played an

outstanding role over history and in the Ummah. They are the women who were specially chosen by Allah to be the wives of the Prophet ﷺ (pbuh).

1.Khadijah bint Khuwaylid ◈ (r.a.)
Lady Khadijah ◈ (r.a.) belonged to the tribe of Quraish and was known as At-Tahirah (the chaste woman) by the people of her tribe. She ◈ (r.a.) had good morals, wisdom and a distinguished character and was the daughter of Khuwaylid ibn Asad ibn 'Abd al-'Uzza, who enjoyed leadership and honour. Her

lineage meets that of the Prophet ﷺ (pbuh) in the fourth grandfather.

Lady Khadijah ◈ (r.a.) married Abu Halah Hind ibn Zararah at-Taymiyy at the age of fifteen. After his death she married 'Atiq ibn 'Abid al-Makhzumiyy. When her second husband passed away she ◈ (r.a.) inherited great wealth and engaged herself in trade. Her wealth was blessed by Allah Almighty and so it increased. She ◈ (r.a.) was informed of Prophet Muhammad's ﷺ (pbuh) good morals and truthfulness and offered him to administer her trade in Syria with her servant Maysarah. The Prophet ﷺ (pbuh) agreed; he had experience in trade as he travelled with his uncle to Syria for trade, and had acquired all the skills and experiences, but above all, trustworthiness and truthfulness in trade. He ﷺ (pbuh) was successful in his trading and returned with great profits which won the heart of Lady Khadijah ◈ (r.a.) and she was highly pleased.

Maysara reported that when he was with the Prophet (pbuh), a cloud formed in the sky above the Prophet ﷺ (pbuh) which moved along as he ﷺ (pbuh) moved, protecting him from the hue of the sun.

Lady Khadijah ﷺ (r.a.) reflected on what the male servant had related to her about the Prophet ﷺ (pbuh) and on what she had heard when she went to a women's gathering. Here a man said, "O women of Quraish! A Prophet is about to rise amongst you. Whoever could marry him, should do so."
Ref: Sahih, Bukhari

The blessed wedding took place between Lady Khadijah ﷺ (r.a.) and the Prophet ﷺ (pbuh), and the first Islamic home was founded on truthfulness and with the pleasure of Allah. Lady Khadijah ﷺ (r.a.) set a supreme example for Muslim women by marrying the Prophet ﷺ (pbuh) for his trustworthiness and honesty, she did not marry for wealth or power nor authority.
Lady Khadijah ﷺ (r.a.) treated the Prophet ﷺ (pbuh) with compassion and affection that relieved his worries. She was a kind and righteous wife who consoled the Prophet (pbuh) in times of adversity. In time, Lady Khadijah ﷺ (r.a.) gave birth to their first blessed daughter Zainab ﷺ (r.a.).

On this joyous occasion many animals were slaughtered and distributed amongst the poor. Soon after Khadija ﷺ (r.a.) gave birth to another blessed daughter Ruqayyah ﷺ (r.a.), and then to blessed Umm Kulthum ﷺ (r.a.). The blessed birth of Fatima Az-Zahra ﷺ (r.a.) took place in the tenth year of their blessed marriage. Lady Khadijah ﷺ (r.a.) also gave birth to two blessed sons, al-Qasim ﷺ (r.a.) and 'Abd Allah ﷺ (r.a.), however both passed away at a young age. Al-Qasim ﷺ (r.a.) was said to have passed away before his second birthday and Abd'Allah ﷺ (r.a.) is reported to have passed away in his childhood.

 ## REVELATION

Prophet Muhammad ﷺ (pbuh) used to meditate in a cave in Mount Hira where the revelation was sent down by Allah ﷻ (Glorified and Exalted) through the arch-angel Jibra'eel ﷺ (a.s.). At this time as was recorded in history, the Prophet ﷺ (pbuh) was forty years of age. Allah Almighty blessed him ﷺ (pbuh) with the light of Prophethood, graced him ﷺ (pbuh) with His message, and sent him ﷺ (pbuh) as a mercy to the worlds (all creations of jinn and men).

The Prophet's ﷺ (pbuh) love for Khadijah ؓ (r.a.) was so intense that he did not marry anyone else whilst he was married to her. Nor did the Prophet ﷺ (pbuh) remarry anyone else until after 2 years of his beloved Khadijah's ؓ (r.a.) passing. Khadijah ؓ (r.a.) was the first woman to accept Islam, she ؓ (r.a.) declared her faith in Islam after the Prophet ﷺ (pbuh) received revelations.

2.Sawda bint Zum'ah ؓ (r.a.)

The Prophet ﷺ (pbuh) married Sawda bint Zum'ah ؓ (r.a.) who was one of the noble ladies of Quraish and who became the second wife of the Prophet ﷺ (pbuh), after Khadijah bint Khuwaylid ؓ (r.a.) had passed away.
She was the daughter of the Quraish tribe Amir bin Lu'ay.
Sawda ؓ (r.a.) and her husband, Sukran ibn 'Amr ؓ (r.a.) had embraced Islam in its early stage. Upon the instruction of the Prophet ﷺ (pbuh), Sawda ؓ (r.a.) and

her husband were amongst the Muslims who migrated to Abyssinia due to persecution by Quraish. They did this in anticipation of Allah's reward.

Her husband soon passed away after their return to Makkah and she began living with her aged father.

Ref: Beloved Wives of The Sublime Messenger

3. A'ishah bint Abi Bakr ﷺ (r.a.)

A'ishah ﷺ (r.a.) is and has been the most knowledgeable woman of the Muslim Ummah according to historical records. She ﷺ (r.a.) was born in Makkah, her father was as-Siddiq ﷺ (r.a.), the Caliph, Abu Bakr Siddiq ﷺ (r.a.) and her mother was known as Umm Ruman ﷺ (r.a.). Naturally being brought up in such a noble house and by honourable parents, A'ishah ﷺ (r.a.) had inherited good morals and compassion from them. The marriage between the Prophet ﷺ (pbuh) and A'ishah ﷺ (r.a.) was based on the command of Allah ﷻ (Glorified and Exalted).

4. Hafsa bint Umar ﷺ (r.a.)

Hafsa bint Umar ﷺ (r.a.) embraced Islam when she was young and was brought up loving Islam, it's teachings and practices. She ﷺ (r.a.) was described as the daughter of the Commander of the

Believers. Her father was 'Umar ibn Khattab ﷺ (r.a.) who became the second Caliph after the Prophet ﷺ (pbuh) had passed away. Hafsa bint 'Umar ﷺ (r.a.) was widowed at a young age, her husband passed away after being injured in the battle of Badr, therefore died a martyr (shaheed).

 ## 5. Zainab bint Khuzayma ﷺ (r.a.)

Zaynab bint Khuzayma ﷺ (r.a.) was born into a noble family from the Banu Hilal tribe in Najd. She ﷺ (r.a.) was given the title Umm al-Masakin (Mother of the poor). She was known for her love for the poor and the orphans. She ﷺ (r.a.) was a woman who loved to do charity and could not bear to see the people hungry and destitute without helping them.
Ref: Al-Haythami, Majma' al-Zawa'id

Zaynab bint Khuzayma ﷺ (r.a.) was the 5th wife of the Prophet ﷺ (pbuh). However, this marriage only lasted for eight months as she ﷺ (r.a.) passed away due to illness and was one of the first wives to be buried in Jannat al-Baqi (burial ground) in Madinah.
Ref: Ibn Sa'd (D 230AH)

6. (Umm Salamah) Hind bint Abi Umayyah ﷺ (r.a.)

A kind and amiable lady, characterised as skilful, intelligent and wise. Her husband was Abdullah ibn Abd-al-Asad Makhzumi, also known as Abu-Salamah ﷺ (r.a.). They were both from the first converts to Islam, and undertook both emigrations of Muslims. Umm Salamah ﷺ (r.a.) was notably the first lady to emigrate to Madinah. Abu Salamah ﷺ (r.a.) was known for his akhlaq (virtue), sadly he was severely injured in the Battle of Uhud and passed away shortly after.

Ref: Hadith-dua-Narrated by Muslim, Abu Dawud, al-Tirmidhi

Umm Salamah ﷺ (r.a.) narrated from her husband Abu Salamah ﷺ (r.a.), that the Prophet ﷺ (pbuh) said: "There is no person who is faced with a calamity and says **"Inna Lillaahi wa inna ilayhi raaji'oon; Allaahumma ajirni fi museebati wakhluf li khayran minha"** (Truly, to Allah we belong and truly to Him we shall return; O Allah, reward me in this calamity and compensate me with something better than it), but Allah ﷻ subhanahu wata'ala will reward him in his calamity and will compensate him with something better than that."

She said: When Abu Salamah ﷺ (r.a.) died, I said what the Messenger of Allah (peace and blessings of Allah be upon him) had commanded me, and Allah compensated me with someone better than him: the Messenger of Allah (peace and blessings of Allah be upon him).

According to another report: when Abu Salamah ﷺ (r.a.) died, I said: Who is better than Abu Salamah, the companion of the Messenger of Allah (peace and blessings of Allah be upon him)? But Allah ﷻ (Glorified and Exalted) decreed that I should say it! Then I got married to the Messenger of Allah (peace and blessings of Allah be upon him).
Ref: Muslim (918)

The Prophet ﷺ (pbuh) proposed to her for marriage, she ﷺ (r.a.) accepted and outlived the Prophet for nearly five decades. Umm Salamah ﷺ (r.a.) lived a long life and was one of the last of the Prophet's ﷺ (pbuh) wives to pass away.

7. Zaynab bint Jahsh ﷺ (r.a.)

Zaynab bint Jahsh ﷺ (r.a.) was the daughter of Jahsh ibn Ri'ab ibn Ya'mur al-Asadiyyah and Umaimah bint Abdul Muttalib bin Hashim from the Banu al-Asad tribe. She ﷺ (r.a.) is also the daughter of the paternal aunt of the Prophet ﷺ (pbuh). A noble, beautiful and intelligent woman, Zaynab bint Jahsh ﷺ (r.a.) was known for her devotion in prayer. She ﷺ (r.a.)

was a divorcee at the time the Prophet ﷺ (pbuh) married her.

8. Juwairiya bint al-Harith ﷺ (r.a.)

She ﷺ (r.a.) was the daughter of al-Hārith ibn Abi Dirar, the chief of Banu (Tribe) Mustaliq. His tribe was defeated in a battle. The Prophet ﷺ (pbuh) freed Juwairiya ﷺ (r.a.) from slavery and married her. This took place after the battle between Banu Mustaliq and the Muslims in Madinah.

Ref: narrated by Ibn Ishaaq with a hasan isnaad. Seerat Ibn Hishaam, 3/408-409.

Hence no woman brought a greater blessing to her people than she did.

9. Ramla bint Abi Sufyan (Umm Habeebah Abi Sufyan) ﷺ (r.a.)

She ﷺ (r.a.) was the daughter of Abu Sufyan ibn Harb. Abu Sufyan ﷺ (r.a.) was the chief of the Umayyad tribe, and a leader of the Quraish. He was also the most powerful opponent of Prophet Muhammad ﷺ (pbuh).

Umm Habeebah 🕌 (r.a.) was married to 'Ubayd-Allah ibn Jahsh, who converted to Christianity and later died in Abyssinia. He attempted to convert her 🕌 (r.a.) to Christianity, but she remained loyal to and steadfast in Islam.

Later she 🕌 (r.a.) married the Prophet 🕌 (pbuh) with a mahr of 400 dinars. It was the Negus (King) of Abyssinia who carried out the ceremony.
Ref:Abu Dawood (2107)

 ## 10. Safiyya bint Huyayy 🕌 (r.a.)

The daughter of Huyayy ibn Akhtab, the chief of the Jewish tribe Banu Nadir. She 🕌 (r.a.) was married to Kinanah who was the leader of Jewish tribe Banu Qurayzah in Khaybar.

The Messenger of Allah 🕌 (pbuh) set Safiyya bint Huyayy free and married her 🕌 (r.a.) after the battle of Khaybar.
Ref: al-Bukhaari (371)

 ## 11. Maimunah bint al-Harith 🕌 (r.a.)

Her 🕌 (r.a.) father was al-Harith ibn Hazn from the Hilal tribe in Makkah. She was originally called Barrah, but Prophet Muhammad 🕌 (pbuh)

changed her name to Maimunah, which means "the blessed".

Maimunah ⁕ (r.a.) was the sister in law of Al-Abbas, the uncle of the Prophet ⁕ (pbuh).

Maimunah ⁕ (r.a.) was married to Mas'ud al-Thaqafi by whom she was later divorced.

✿ Chapter 5 ✿

The Prophetic Household - Ahl al-Bayt

 The Blessed Beloved Daughters of Prophet
 (pbuh)

The Prophet ﷺ (pbuh) had 4 daughters with his beloved wife Lady Khadijah Bint Khuwaylid ⚘ (r.a.). They were in chronological order, Lady Zainab ⚘ (r.a.), Lady Ruqaiyyah ⚘ (r.a.), Lady Umm Kulthum ⚘ (r.a.), and Lady Faatimah ⚘ (r.a.).

The first 3 daughters passed away before the Prophet ﷺ, except for Lady Faatimah ⚘ (r.a.), who passed away 6 months after the Prophet ﷺ (pbuh). Just like their beloved father, the blessed daughters were not free from their share of trials and tribulations. The Prophet ﷺ (pbuh) also had sons who unfortunately passed away at a very early age. The eldest daughter of the Prophet ﷺ (pbuh), Sayyidah Zainab ⚘ (r.a.), was born 10 years before the Prophet ﷺ (pbuh) received Prophethood. She was married to her aunt's son named Abu al-As ibn al-Rabi'. The second daughter Sayyidah Ruqaiyyah ⚘ (r.a.) was married to 'Utbah and the 3rd daughter Umm Kulthum ﷺ (r.a.) was married to 'Utaybah; both were the sons of Abu Lahab. Abu Lahab was one of the uncles of the Prophet (pbuh).

When prophethood was declared, and he ﷺ (pbuh) started propagating (spreading) Islam, Abu Lahab's great love for his then beloved nephew Prophet Muhammad ﷺ (pbuh), turned into hatred. This was because he disliked Islam.

So he told his sons to divorce their wives - the daughters of the Prophet ﷺ (pbuh). His sons were given an ultimatum that they should divorce the Prophet's ﷺ (pbuh) daughters Lady Ruqaiyyah ﷺ (r.a.) and Lady Umm Kulthum ﷺ (r.a.) or lose ties with their father Abu Lahab and their mother. However Abu al-As ibn al-Rabi' who wasn't amongst the angry people of Makkah, (those against Islam), refused to divorce Lady Zainab ﷺ (r.a.).

Lady Ruqaiyya ﷺ (r.a.) then married Uthman bin 'Affan ﷺ (r.a.). Later, she fell ill and passed away. The Prophet ﷺ (pbuh) married off his other daughter Umm Kulthum ﷺ (r.a.) to Uthman bin Affan ﷺ (r.a.).

Prophet Muhammad ﷺ (pbuh) loved Uthman bin 'Affan ﷺ (r.a.); one of the most modest of the companions, so much so that after the passing of Lady Umm Kulthum, who was married to Uthman bin 'Affan ﷺ (r.a.), Prophet ﷺ (pbuh) said that if he had another daughter he would marry her off to him too.

Many years later after Abu al-As ibn al-Rabi' became a Muslim and retained the marriage to Lady Zainab ﷺ (r.a.), they were blessed with the birth of a son and a daughter. Their son was named 'Ali who passed away in his infancy, their daughter Lady Umamah ﷺ (r.a.) lived on as a cousin to Al Husein ﷺ (r.a.) and Al Hasan ﷺ (r.a.).

For the Prophet ﷺ (pbuh) his grandchildren were the coolness of his eyes. He ﷺ (pbuh) was so fond of Umamah ﷺ (r.a.) that he would carry her to the masjid, keep her in his arms and make salaah with her in his blessed arms. The boys grew up with Lady Umamah ﷺ (r.a.) who was older than them, so they were used to being around her.

✿Family – Ancestral Lineage of Rasulullah salallahu alayhi wasallam

Wath'ila ibn al-Asqa' said Rasulullah ﷺ (pbuh) said:
"Allah chose Isma'il from the children of Ibrahim and He chose the Banu Kinana (Kinana Tribe) from the children of Isma'il.
He chose the Quraish from the Banu Kinana and He chose the Banu Hashim (Tribe of Hashim) from the Quraish. He chose me from the Banu Hashim."
Ref: Al Tirmidhi and Muslim
Al-'Abbas said that the Prophet ﷺ (pbuh) said:
"Allah created creations and He placed me among the best of them from the best of their generations. Then He selected the tribes and He put me among the best tribe. Then He selected the families, and He put me among the best of the families. I am the best of them in person and the best of them in family."
Ref: Al Bayhaki and Al-Timidhi

Clearly the Prophet Muhammad ﷺ (pbuh) was the chosen one; 'Al-Mustafa', whom Allah has commanded us to support and honour throughout our lifetime.

❀The Importance of the family of the Prophet Muhammad ﷺ (pbuh)

Allah ﷻ (Glorified and Exalted) specially chose His Prophet Muhammad ﷺ (pbuh) over all creations and honoured him with all the unique attributes, abilities and miraculous capabilities through Allah's blessings. Allah also gave high rank to the descendants of the Prophet Muhammad ﷺ (pbuh) and raised the position of the people who are related to and dependant on him ﷺ (pbuh). In addition, Allah Almighty has made it a must for the ummah to love the entire family and progeny of the Prophet ﷺ (pbuh) *(Ref: Ash-Shifa of Qadi 'Iyad)*, and made it a duty on all Muslims to know and acknowledge the noble status, to speak with honour, to be gracious, to respect and to have supreme love for the family and the progeny of the Prophet ﷺ (pbuh) for the sake of Allah. This is paramount in order to protect the sanctity of the Prophet ﷺ (pbuh) through his family and progeny by knowing them in all forms of reverence.

Imam Abu Hanifa had great respect for the descendants of the Prophet ﷺ (pbuh) (lineage from the Prophetic household). He would seek closeness to Allah

Almighty by spending on those who made their lineage known as well as those who concealed it.   It is reported that once Imam Abu Hanifa gave 12,000 dirhams to someone from the lineage of the Prophet ﷺ (pbuh) who concealed his identity and urged his companions to do the same.
Ref: Collection of 40 Hadith al arba'in - Muhammad ibn Jaffar Al-Kattani - on the duty of loving the noble family of the Prophet Muhammad (pbuh))

Al Bukhari reported in a hadith of Ibn Umar ﷺ (r.a.) – "be vigilant on the outlook of Muhammad ﷺ (pbuh) and the people of his house", meaning: "protect them, do not harm or hurt them and do not behave in a disrespectful and contemptuous manner towards them".

Imam as-Shafi'i said in a poem:

O mounted one, stop at Al-Muhassab at Mina and
rejoice in the one who is tranquil at its Khayf
and the one who is energetic, and the fore-dawn
when the Hajjis pour forth to Mina, pouring
forth like the clash of the overflowing gulf.
If love of the family of Muhammad is shi'ism
(rafidi), then let both jinn and mankind bear
witness that I am a shi'i (rafidi).

*Ref: Collection of 40 Hadith al arba'in - Muhammad ibn Jaffar Al-
Kattani - on the duty of loving the noble family of the Prophet
Muhammad (pbuh))*

When Imam as-Shafi'i was accused of being shi'i because of his immense love for the Prophet Muhammad's ﷺ (pbuh) household (family); he would reply in a poem:

"I continued in concealment until it was as if I was dumb to return and answer to the question about you.

In order for me and you to be safe from the words of the critics.

You are safe, and is any area of the people safe?"

Imam As-Shafi'i also wrote the following:

"O Household of Allah's Messenger!
Love for you is a duty from Allah
In the Qur'an He sent down
[High glory is yours
And he who has no relation with you,
Has no prayer].

Ref: Collection of 40 Hadith al arba'in - Muhammad ibn Jaffar Al-Kattani - on the duty of loving the noble family of the Prophet Muhammad (pbuh))

Suffice to say that all the imams of the four schools of thoughts, namely, Imam Malik, Imam Abu Hanifa, Imam As-Shafi'i and Imam Ahmad ibn Hanbal taught and portrayed respect and love for the family of the Prophet ﷺ (pbuh).

Thus, as professed Muslims, we must expect ourselves to follow the noble examples of those noble imams in our duty of loving the family of Prophet Muhammad ﷺ (pbuh). This will earn us closeness to Allah and His beloved Messenger ﷺ (pbuh

Chapter 6

BATTLES - Treaty of Hudaibiyyah, Battle of Badr, Battle of Uhud.

The Prophet Muhammad ﷺ (pbuh) fought a few battles of which he led. He ﷺ (pbuh) was always the commander of the army. To mention some of the battles, they are:

- Treaty of Hudaibiyyah
- Battle of Badr
- Battle of Uhud
- Battle of Trench
- Battle of Muta
- Battle of Hunayn
- Campaign of Tabuk

Let us explore one of the battles:

 The Battle of Badr.
FACTS:
- It took place on the 17th of Ramadan in the

2nd year of Hijra (the year of migration).
- It was between the polytheists of Makkah (Mecca) and the Muslims.
- Muslims were outnumbered by a ratio of 1:3
- 313 Muslims ill-equipped / the enemies were around 1,000 well equipped
- Allah Almighty sent down thousands of angels to help the Muslims achieve victory over the Quraish.
- 14 companions were martyred.

Hence, it has become a tradition for many muslims around the world to commemorate the battle of Badr on the 17th of every Ramadhan. Needless to say the Prophet ﷺ (pbuh) was the leader of the army, leading and organising the muslim soldiers.

The common procedure practiced in battles in Arabia was to recite praises and achievements of their leaders during battles in order to keep the spirits high towards achieving victory.

In this battle, Utbah ibn Rabiah, Shaybah ibn Rabiah, and Walid ibn Utbah stepped out of line and insulted the muslims. Three youths from the Ansar namely Awf ibn Harith, Muawwiyah ibn Harith and Abdullah ibn Rawda displayed bravery in opposing them.
In this situation the Prophet ﷺ (pbuh) chose his uncle Hamzah, 'Ubayda ibn Harith and 'Ali ibn Abi Talib to go forward and face the enemies. This combat between them did not last long as all the three (mentioned above) from the enemy's side were killed whilst 'Ubayda ibn Harith was badly wounded. Just before he passed away at the battlefield, he asked the Prophet ﷺ (pbuh), "am I not a martyr (shaheed) O messenger of Allah?" The Prophet ﷺ (pbuh) replied, "indeed you are."
Ref: Seerah of the final Prophet ﷺ Hasan Al banna

In one incident, a companion named Sawad ibn Ghaziyah deliberately stepped out of line within the row of armies to attract the attention of the the Prophet ﷺ (pbuh). In turn the Prophet ﷺ (pbuh) poked him lightly with a stick to step back into line.

[Ref: Tarikh al-Tabari Vol 2, P 446]

It is worth mentioning the immense and devoted love the companions and all those involved in all the battles had for the Prophet ﷺ (pbuh). They were all willing to be martyrs.

This is sincere love for the Prophet ﷺ (pbuh) that we should always take into account and have as examples in our lives. Our love for the Prophet Muhammad Rasulullah sallallahu 'alaihi wasallam (pbuh) must not only be restricted to lip service; but rather we should have sincerity in our hearts leading us to put our love into actions by obeying the teachings of the Prophet ﷺ (pbuh) and loving those whom the Prophet ﷺ (pbuh) loves and commands us to love.

The companions of the Prophet ﷺ (pbuh) included both young and old individuals.
There was a young sahabah (companion) of the Prophet ﷺ (pbuh) named Umayr, a 16year old boy who flung some dates that he was eating into the air. Whilst eating the dates he cried out, "these are holding me back from paradise." He then joined the battle and fought until he died as a martyr (shaheed).

The enemies from the Quraish suffered great losses. It is in this battle of Badr that Abu Jahl, the arch enemy of the Prophet ﷺ (pbuh) died at the hands of the two youths from the tribe of the Ansar. This is also the battle whereby Allah ﷻ (Glorified and Exalted) answered the Prophet's ﷺ (pbuh) supplications which were revealed in the Quran in Surah Al Anfal (8 verse 9-10)

اِذْ تَسْتَغِيثُوْنَ رَبَّكُمْ فَاسْتَجَابَ لَكُمْ اَنِّىْ مُمِدُّكُمْ بِاَلْفٍ مِّنَ الْمَلٰئِكَةِ مُرْدِفِيْنَ

وَمَا جَعَلَهُ اللّٰهُ اِلَّا بُشْرٰى وَلِتَطْمَئِنَّ بِهٖ قُلُوْبُكُمْ ۚ وَمَا النَّصْرُ اِلَّا مِنْ عِنْدِ اللّٰهِ ۗ اِنَّ اللّٰهَ عَزِيْزٌ حَكِيْمٌ

When you sought help of your lord and He answered you: "I will help you with a thousand of the angels each behind the other in successions." Allah made it only as glad tidings, and that your hearts be at rest therewith. And there is no victory except from Allah. Verily, Allah is Almighty, All Wise.

52

Therewith, the Muslims were blessed by Allah ﷻ (Glorified and Exalted) with the help of the angels who had received instructions from Allah ﷻ (Glorified and Exalted) against the enemies.

Whilst all the believers in the battle felt the presence of the angels only a few of them witnessed the presence of the angels visibly and audibly. The angels were led by the Archangel Jibra'eel عليه السلام (a.s.). In one instance a believer from the army of the Prophet ﷺ (pbuh), whilst pursuing a man from the enemy, before he could reach him, witnessed the man's head flying off having been struck by an unseen hand. In other instances some of the few companions had brief glimpses of the angels sent by Allah the Exalted.

Such is the victory of those who have strong and sincere faith and rely upon the help of only Allah Almighty. A great example taught to us by the most noble Prophet Muhammad ﷺ (pbuh).

There were many victorious moments achieved by the Prophet ﷺ (pbuh) with the help of Allah Lord of the worlds.

With Imaan and Taqwa - there is no failure
with Allah except success. When you have
Allah with you, you have success.

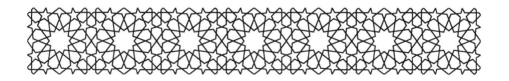

❧ Chapter 7 ❧

The Night Journey -Al-'Isra' wal-Mi'raj
The meeting of The Prophet ﷺ (pbuh) with Allah.

 Al-'Isra' wal-Mi'raj - the 'journey' (isra) and the 'ascension' (mi'raj)

This event took place on the night of the 27th of Rajab. The Prophet ﷺ (pbuh) was resting at the Ka'ba one night, with his uncle and his cousin by his side. He ﷺ (pbuh) felt tranquility and peace at this special place of worship.

Not long after the Prophet ﷺ (pbuh) had fallen asleep, he ﷺ (pbuh) was woken up by Jibra'eel عليه السلام (a.s.), who was accompanied by Mikaeel عليه السلام (a.s.) and Israfeel عليه السلام (a.s.). Certainly, no one sees the angels except Rasulullah (messenger) ﷺ (pbuh). The angels had been sent by Almighty Allah.

The angels carried the Prophet ﷺ (pbuh) to the spring of zamzam where they asked him ﷺ (pbuh) to lie on his blessed back. Jibra'eel عليه السلام (a.s.) led the way and instructed Mikaeel عليه السلام (a.s.) who followed his orders. First, Jibra'eel عليه السلام (a.s.) split open the Prophet's ﷺ chest from the throat down to his belly. Then Jibra'eel عليه السلام (a.s.) said to Mikaeel عليه السلام (a.s.) "bring me a vessel (usually made of copper) of water from zamzam (blessed spring water) so that I may purify his heart and expand his breast (chest)". Of course Jibra'eel عليه السلام (a.s.) had asked for zamzam water so that he could wash our Beloved Prophet's ﷺ (pbuh) heart with it and he washed it three times. Mikaeel عليه السلام (a.s.) carried the vessel back and forth with fresh zamzam water each time that Jibra'eel عليه السلام (a.s.) washed the blessed heart of the Prophet ﷺ (pbuh).

Eventually, Mikaeel عليه السلام (a.s.) brought to Jibra'eel عليه السلام (a.s.) a golden vessel filled with wisdom and belief which Jibra'eel عليه السلام (a.s.) emptied into the chest of the Prophet ﷺ (pbuh). Jibra'eel عليه السلام (a.s.) filled the Prophet's ﷺ (pbuh) heart with forbearance, knowledge, certainty, best of character - incompatible to any other human beings. Jibra'eel عليه السلام (a.s.) then miraculously closed the Prophet's ﷺ (pbuh) chest and sealed it with the Seal of

Prophethood which was between the shoulders of the Prophet ﷺ (pbuh).

Then, a strange animal was brought into the presence of the Prophet ﷺ (pbuh). It was the Buraaq: a creature described as handsome faced and bridled, a tall and white
beast, bigger than a donkey but smaller than a mule. It had long ears and two wings on its thighs which gave
strength to its legs. At first the Buraaq seemed to show resistance when the Prophet ﷺ (pbuh) was going
to mount it. However, when the angel Jibra'eel ﷺ (a.s.) put his hand on its mane and said: quote - "are you not ashamed (O Buraaq)? By Allah, none has mounted you in all creation dearer to Allah than he." Hearing this the Buraaq was so ashamed that it sweated until it became soaked, and it stood still so that the Prophet ﷺ (pbuh) mounted it." - unquote.

Ref: The Prophet's ﷺ night journey and heavenly ascent by Sayyid Muhammad Ibn Alawi Al-Maliki

It had been reported that other Prophets (alayhi mussalaam - peace be upon them a.s.) in the past used to ride the Buraaq. Quote - "Sa'eed Ibn Al-Musayyib said: it is the beast of Ibrahim ﷺ (a.s.) which he used to mount whenever he travelled to the sacred house." -

unquote. Therefore it is very clear that the Buraaq felt very honoured to be mounted by the most dearest Prophet of Allah ﷺ (pbuh).

As they prepared to set off on this wondrous journey into the brilliant night sky filled with stars, the angel Jibra'eel عليه السلام (a.s.) positioned himself on the right side of the Prophet Muhammad ﷺ (pbuh) holding the stirrup of the Buraaq, while Mikaeel عليه السلام (a.s.) was on the left side holding the reigns. Soon they were ascending - past the clouds, past the bright stars, deeper into the night.

During the journey they descended at specific places where the Messenger ﷺ (pbuh) of Allah said his prayers. The first stop was at Yathrib - land of migration (Madinah), second stop was at Madyan at the tree of Musa عليه السلام (a.s.), third stop was at Mountain of Sinaa' where Allah had addressed Prophet Musa عليه السلام (a.s.), fourth stop was at Bayt La'hm, where I'sa ibn Maryam عليه السلام a.s. (Jesus son of Mary) was born. Finally, they reached Masjid Al-Aqsa in Jerusalem where the Prophet Muhammad ﷺ (pbuh) miraculously led all the Prophets عليهم السلام (a.s.) of the past in prayer.

As they continued the journey and while the Prophet ﷺ (pbuh) was travelling on the Buraaq, he saw a devil with fire and recited the following du'a:

I seek refuge in Allah's blessed face
and in Allah's perfect words
which neither the righteous nor the disobedient overstep
from evil that descends from the heaven
and evil that ascends to it
and evil that is created in the earth
and the trials of night and day
and the visitors of night and day
save the visitor that visits goodness upon us,
O Beneficent One'

During this miraculous journey, the Prophet ﷺ (pbuh) witnessed several fascinating events. He ﷺ (pbuh) saw how people reaped their harvest based on what they sowed on earth. He ﷺ (pbuh) saw the Al-Mujahideen (people who strive through their lives with their wealth and lifestyles in the path of Allah Almighty) being rewarded for their good deeds. For every single good deed that they did, it was multiplied for them seven hundred times and for everything that they spent was being returned to them in multitude. Such is the reward of Allah, The Most Generous.

Prophet Muhammad ﷺ (pbuh) also experienced the fragrant wind that carried the scent of the lady who combed the hair of Pharaoh's daughter. She was the blessed woman who was killed together with her husband and children for declaring her belief in Allah against Pharaoh (Fir'awn). Pharaoh claimed himself to be God. Once when the comb fell to the floor, while combing Fir'awn's daughter's hair, she said: "Bismillah ta'isa fir'awn - in the name of Allah, perish fir'awn!" At hearing this Fir'awn's daughter asked her if she has another lord other than her father and if she should tell her father. To this the lady bravely said, "yes".

This event tells us and teaches us to be steadfast in our belief in Allah as the one and only God to be worshipped.

On the other hand, the Prophet ﷺ (pbuh) also witnessed the punishment of people whose heads were being repeatedly crushed. The Angel Gabriel (Jibra'eel) عليه السلام (a.s.) told the Prophet ﷺ (pbuh) that those were the people who were lazy and did not get up from their slumber to fulfil their obligatory prayers. And then there was the punishment of the people who failed to perform their obligatory charity - zakaat. They were eating fruits shaped like the heads of devils, from a tree that grows in hell: and hot coals and stones of the hellfire. There were several other punishments for different types of disobedience to Allah's commands. For example, those who were dealing with interest (usury), devouring the rights of orphans, those who slander people and many other forms of punishments that were witnessed by the Prophet ﷺ (pbuh).

Remarkably on the contrary, there are always the good tidings of Paradise. As The Prophet ﷺ (pbuh) and Jibra'eel عليه السلام (a.s.) continued with their miraculous journey, they came across a valley that breathed a breeze of sweet cool fragrance with musk. The Prophet ﷺ (pbuh) heard a voice and asked Jibra'eel عليه السلام (a.s.) about it. It was the voice of Paradise saying:

"O my Lord, bring me what You have promised me!
Too abundant are my rooms, my gold-laced garments,
My silk, my brocades, my carpets, my pearls, my corals,
My silver, my gold, my goblets, my bowls, my pitchers,
My couches, my honey, my water, my milk, my wine!

 And the Lord says:

You shall have every single Muslim man and woman,
Every believing man and woman,
Everyone who has believed in Me and My Messengers
And did excellent deeds
Without associating a partner with Me
Nor taking helpers without Me!
Anyone who fears Me shall be safe,
And whoever asks of Me, I shall give him,
And whoever loans Me something, I shall repay him,
And whoever relies upon Me, I shall suffice him!
I am Allah beside Whom there is no God.
I never fail in My promise.

{Successful indeed are the believers.} (Qur'an 23:1)
{So blessed be Allah, the best of Creators!}
(Qur'an23:14)

 "And Paradise answers: I accept."

Ref: The Prophet's ﷺ night journey and heavenly ascent by Sayyid Muhammad Ibn Alawi Al-Maliki

As they continued on with their journey, they came to another valley; here the Prophet ﷺ (pbuh) experienced hearing a repulsive voice accompanied by very foul-smelling air. The angel Jibra'eel ﷺ (a.s.) informed the Prophet ﷺ (pbuh) that this voice was the sound of hellfire saying to Allah. Quote: "O Lord, give me what you promised me! Abundant are my chains, my yokes, my punishments, my fires, my thistles, my pus, my tortures!
My depth is abysmal, my heat unbearable'
Therefore give me what You promised me!" unquote.

Allah then replied to hellfire as follows:

"You shall have every idolater and idolatress,

Every disbelieving man and woman, every foul one, and every tyrant who does not believe in the Day of Reckoning'".

Al-Dajjal (the Anti-Christ) was also shown to the Prophet ﷺ (pbuh) in his actual form. The Prophet ﷺ (pbuh) described him as being the size of a mammoth. His skin was pale and white, and one of his eyes protruded and he had hair like the branches of a tree.

The Prophet ﷺ (pbuh) also saw the column of Islam being carried by the Angels. This appeared to be in the form of a white column made of magnificent pearls. Later, the Prophet ﷺ (pbuh) heard a voice calling him from his right. The voice was calling his name, "Muhammad", desiring his attention. The Prophet ﷺ (pbuh) ignored it, then Jibra'eel عليه السلام (a.s.) informed the Prophet ﷺ (pbuh) that it was the call of the Jews; and should he had responded to the call his community would have followed Judaism.

As they continued with their journey the Prophet ﷺ (pbuh) heard someone else calling him. This time from his left. Again, the voice demanded attention from the Prophet ﷺ (pbuh) on the pretext to ask about something. Again, the Prophet ﷺ (pbuh) ignored it. At

this point the Prophet ﷺ (pbuh) was informed by Jibra'eel عليه السلام (a.s.) that it was the call of the Christians. Had the Prophet ﷺ (pbuh) responded, his Ummah (followers) would have followed the religion of Christianity.
(Ref: The Prophets night journey and heavenly ascent -Syed Muhammad Ibn Alawi Al-Maliki)

Likewise, the Prophet ﷺ (pbuh) was allowed to witness several other events involving rewards of good deeds and paradise. These events are important and encouraging for us to know about; and we can obtain this knowledge by reading the book on Al-'Isra' wal-Mi'raj.

As they continued their ascent to the seven heavens, they stopped at each level of the heavens and were greeted and welcomed by other Prophets. As they reached the first heaven, Jibra'eel عليه السلام (a.s.) asked for it to be opened. A voice said, "Who is it?" upon which Jibra'eel عليه السلام (a.s.) replied, "Jibra'eel." Then the voice said, "Who is with you?", and he replied, "Muhammad." The voice further asked, "Was he sent for?", to which Jibra'eel عليه السلام (a.s.) replied, "He was sent for." The door opened, and Adam عليه السلام (a.s.) greeted the Prophet ﷺ (pbuh) and prayed for him.

They then continued to the second heaven, where a voice asked the same questions and Jibra'eel عليه السلام (a.s.) gave the same answers. When the door opened, the Prophet ﷺ (pbuh) was greeted by Prophet I'sa ibn Maryam (Jesus son of Mary عليه السلام peace be upon him), and Prophet Yahya ibn Zakariya (John عليه السلام peace be upon him). They welcomed Prophet Muhammad ﷺ (pbuh) and prayed for him.

At the third heaven the same happened and the door was opened. It was Yusuf (Joseph عليه السلام peace be upon him) who prayed for Rasulullah (messenger of Allah ﷺ pbuh). At the fourth heaven the Prophet ﷺ (pbuh) was welcomed by Prophet Idris (Enoch عليه السلام peace be upon him) who prayed for him. The same happened at the fifth heaven, the door opened and it was Prophet Harun (Aaron عليه السلام peace be upon him), and at the sixth heaven, Prophet Musa (Moses عليه السلام peace be upon him) who welcomed and prayed for the Prophet ﷺ (pbuh). At the seventh heaven the Prophet ﷺ (pbuh) was greeted by Prophet Ibrahim (Abraham عليه السلام peace be upon him) and was shown the Frequented House (Al-Bayt Al-Ma'mur). The house where seventy angels enter everyday.

After this blissful event Jibra'eel عليه السلام (a.s.) showed Rasulullah (messenger of Allah ﷺ pbuh) the Lote-tree of the Furthest Limit, known as the Sidrat al-Muntahā - the most important part of the journey on this night. At reaching this point, Jibra'eel الَعَلَيْهِ (a.s.) told Rasulullah (messenger of Allah ﷺ pbuh) that he had to travel on his own across this bridge to meet with Allah Almighty, his Lord. This is because even Arch Angel Gabriel (Jibra'eel) was not privileged to cross Sidrat al-Muntaha whereby his wings would be burned.

Ref: Muhammad messenger of Allah ash-shifa of qadi'iyad

This is the most enlightening moment of this auspicious journey of ascension to the seven heavens. It was the time when Allah ﷻ (Glorified and Exalted) dispensed of His greatest gifts As-salaah (the 50 prayers which were later reduced to 5 daily prayers) to Rasulullah ﷺ (pbuh) and his followers. Ibn Hazm and Anas bin Malik narrated that the Prophet ﷺ (pbuh) said that Allah ﷻ (Glorified and Exalted) had enjoined fifty prayers on the ummah (nation of the Prophet ﷺ pbuh). When Rasulullah (messenger of Allah ﷺ pbuh) returned with this order of Allah, and he passed by Musa الَعَلَيْهِ (a.s.) who asked him, *quote:* "What has Allah enjoined on your followers?' Rasulullah (messenger of Allah ﷺ pbuh) replied, 'He has enjoined fifty prayers on them'. Musa الَعَلَيْهِ (a.s.) said, 'Go back to your Lord (and appeal for reduction) for your followers will not be able to bear

it." **unquote**. At this, the Prophet ﷺ (pbuh) returned to his Lord, and asked for a reduction, the prayers were reduced to 45. When passing by Musa عليه السلام (a.s.) again, Musa عليه السلام (a.s.) said, 'Go back to your Lord as your followers will not be able to bear it.' The Prophet Muhammad ﷺ (pbuh) returned to Allah عز وجل (Glorified and Exalted) and asked for a further reduction; this time the prayer was reduced to 40. This happened over and over again until the prayer was reduced to 5. Our beloved Rasulullah (messenger of Allah ﷺ pbuh) went back and forth to Allah عز وجل (Glorified and Exalted) several times to ask for a reduction to our daily prayers.
Ref: Sahih Bukhari

Everytime, when descending through the seven heavens on the way back to earth, Prophet Muhammad ﷺ (pbuh) passed by Prophet Musa عليه السلام (a.s.) who kept saying, "go back".

This is a beautiful display of the Prophet's ﷺ (pbuh) love for his ummah (followers) and of Allah's عز وجل (Glorified and Exalted) love for His beloved. This night of majesty and greatness outweighs all other nights, filled with nobility and radiance, when the beloved met with his Creator.

Epilogue

A millennium, centuries and decades have passed, yet the virtues and teachings of the most excellent and best creation of God Almighty who has ever walked on the face of this earth, have never ceased to exist in the hearts, minds and lives of mankind. That man is no other than the most beloved Prophet and Messenger of God; Muhammad ﷺ (peace and blessings be upon him).

Qur'an: Chapter 21:107 - (Surah Al Anbiya)
"And we have sent to you (O'Muhammad ﷺ pbuh) not but as a mercy to the worlds (mankind, jinns and all that exists)."

اللَّهُمَّ صَلِّ عَلَى مُحَمَّدٍ وَعَلَى آلِ مُحَمَّدٍ

O Allah! Send Your blessing to (the prophet) Muhammad and the progeny of Muhammad".

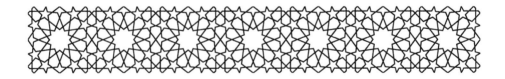

71

Glossary

- ﷻ – Subhanahu wa Ta'ala (Glorified and Exalted)
- ﷺ – salallahu alayhi wasallam (peace and blessing be upon him)
- pbuh – peace be upon him
- ﵂ – (r.a.) radiallahu anha (female) (May Allah be pleased with her)
- ﵁ – (r.a.) radiallahu anhu (male) (May Allah be pleased with him)
- ﵌ – (a.s.) alayhis salaam (peace be upon him) (singular)
- ﵇ – (a.s.) alayhi mussalam (peace be upon them) (plural)
- Prophet Moses – (Prophet Musa in the Qur'an)
- Bani Israel – The Children of Israel (People of Moses)
- Aam ul Fil – the year of the elephant
- Adaab – correct mannerisms, inward and outward
- Buraaq – creature on which the Prophet ﷺ made his night journey – al Isra wal Miraj
- Fajr – morning prayer which is said at dawn, first light

- Sujood – prostration
- Wudu' – ablution (parts of the body that Muslims wash before standing in prayer).

ᎶᏇ**Quiz** ᎶᏇ

1. What is salawat?

2. When and where was the Prophet ﷺ (pbuh) born?

3. Who was the first woman to accept Islam?

4. At what age did the Prophet ﷺ (pbuh) receive the revelation?

5. Which of the Prophets ﷺ (pbuh) beloved daughters was married to Uthman bin Affan ﷺ?

6. What is the meaning of Al-Mustafa?

7. What is the etiquette of drinking water?

8. Which battle took place on the 17th of Ramadhan?

9. Which angel accompanied the Prophet ﷺ (pbuh) on his night journey?

10. Which Prophet did they meet on the 5th heaven?

Bibliography

The Burda
Imam Sharaf Ad-Din Al-Busiri

The Morning of Light
Al Karma Publications

Prophetic Biography Seerat Diya' Al-Nabi
Book: The Morning of Light

Al-Khasais al-Kubra with reference to Abu Nu'aym from ibn 'Abbās
Radi Allahu Anhu

Sahih Muslim

Al Tirmidhi

Al Bukhari and Muslim

Hafidh Sam'aani, Adaab al-Imala wal-Istimla

Bukhari; Sahih

Imam Malik and Abu Daud

Bukhari

Abu Daud

Sahih, Bukhari

Beloved Wives of The Sublime Messenger, M I H Pirzada,
Al Karam Publications

Al-Haythami, Majma' al-Zawa'id

Ibn Sa'd (D 230AH),
Book - Kitab al-Tabaqat al-Kabir Vol10

Hadith-dua-Narrated by Muslim, Abu Dawud, al-Tirmidhi

Al Tirmidhi
Book Sunan Al Tirmidhi, Book of al-Da'awat

Muslim (918)

Narrated by Ibn Ishaaq with a hasan isnaad. Seerat Ibn Hishaam,
3/408-409.

Abu Dawood (2107)

al-Bukhaari (371)

Al Tirmidhi and Muslim

Al Bayhaki and Al-Timidhi

Ash-Shifa of Qadi 'Iyad

Collection of 40 Hadith al arba'in - Muhammad ibn Jaffar Al-Kattani - on the duty of loving the noble family of the Prophet Muhammad (pbuh))

Seerah of the final Prophet ﷺ Hasan Al banna

Tarikh al-Tabari Vol 2, P 446

Al Qur'an

The Prophets night journey and heavenly ascent -Syed Muhammad Ibn Alawi Al-Maliki

Muhammad messenger of Allah ash-shifa of qadi'iyad

Sahih Bukhari

*The Burda
Imam Sharaf Ad-Din Al-Busiri*

O you who are the greatest sign for the one able to perceive,
And the most sublime blessing for the one desiring benefit"

Ref: The Burda, Imam Sharaf Ad-Din Al-Busiri